Hell Hath No Fury
Like A Woman Scorned

101 poems

by

Jan Price

A BBTS Publication
Deri, Bargoed.
BBTS (Baarbaara The Sheep Publications)
Est. Feb 2012
email: **baarbaarathesheep@hotmail.co.uk**
baarbaarathesheep/wordpress.com

Baarbaara
The Sheep

ISBN-13: 9798415851393

Imprint: Independently published

KDP Assigned ISBN registered with Booksinprint.com

Editor: Bourke A. Le Carpentier

Front Cover Design: Ian Ellery KindaMagic.Co.UK

Typeset: Times New Roman

Acknowledgement.

I would like to thank my friend Bourke Le Carpentier for his tireless support in helping me put this book together, editing, correcting and his great suggestions. I could not have done it without him. In my life as a landlady and licensee I have been privileged to know some amazing people and Bourke and his lovely wife Joan are such people. I cannot thank them enough for their time and patience.

Foreword

Jan Price has an incredibly inventive imagination. She enthusiastically, and seemingly with little effort, writes on such a diverse range of subject matter, finding appropriate terms and expressions germane to the subject in hand. For instance, Anne the Arsonist describes her ex-boyfriend as an old flame. The vampire comes home to dinner, "Oh, not *stake* again?" It goes on and on. I find myself chuckling uncontrollably here and there while browsing about in her writings.

She must have downloaded the entire content of Roger's, and Brewer's Phrase & Fable into her head, as I'm sure Shakespeare, Wordsworth, Yeats, and all would have been astonished at the diversity of her creativity even though their styles are poles apart.

She is so refreshingly uninhibited, describing without a qualm, the details of lady's underwear and how to turn a man on and off, but without the slightest intimation of porn. She has a comic imagination that can actually render this jaded reader flabbergasted. She is so astonishingly inventive that it is impossible to compete with her eloquence.

Bourke A. Le Carpentier
Immediate past president of the Aberdare & District
Chamber of Trade & Commerce.

Contents

0 Hell Hath No Fury Like a Woman Scorned

The wind was a'wailing and screaming
As if it had a mania.
The moon was a trailing ghost ship
Down in Transylvania.

The road was a ribbon of moonlight
Over the purple moor,
When the vampire came home early
Up to his castle door.

"Let me in," he shouted,
"Come wife open the portal,
For I must get back in my coffin
If I'm to remain immortal."

"Come open up my lovely
You're the best wife in the land."
And open up she did at once
With the rolling pin in her hand.

"Where the hell have you been all night?
I'm sick of these late hours.
While I have to stay in this morbid place
Watching from the towers."

"You never think of taking me out,
Oh you never consider me.
It's not like when we first married.
Fangs ain't what they used to be."

"You promised me new furniture.
Said you'd decorate the crypt.
And in the mausoleum,
The curtains are all ripped."

"And there's all these droppings to clean up,
From your bloody bats
And in each and every corner
There are spiders, toads and rats."

"You never offer to do repairs.
You are so very crafty.
This castle's old and very cold
And every room is draughty."

Drac took off his cloak, said to his wife,
"Stop nagging and get dinner,
I'm the one who has to work.
I'm the main blood winner."

"Times are tough my nagging wife.
I try to do my share,
But modern medicine's caught up with us.
There's no more Burke and Hare."

"I can't get rid of the bodies now,
Tell me what you'd like me to do?
I'm the one who's out all night,
Working my fangs to the roots for you."

His wife brandished the rolling pin
"I've had enough," she said.
"And I haven't finished anyway
So don't sneak off to bed."

"You never help me in the kitchen.
What more is there to say.
I wish it was all right for me
To sleep all ruddy day."

"I'm stuck here with the cleaning

This huge amount of dirt.
I've tried every washing powder going,
To get the blood out of your shirt."

"Why can't I have a Hoover
To clean up every room.
I cannot go much longer
With just a witch's broom."

"This place is so old fashioned,
Nothing's automatic.
What other wife would put up with
Those corpses in the attic?"

"The things I had before we met
Are nearly now diminished.
Don't you dare change into a bat
And fly off before I'm finished."

"Every one of my relatives,
You know, that you did wrong to.
But they're a better class of family
Than the zombies you belong to."

"I know you don't like mummy
And you say that she's a wreck,
And you can't get through the bandages
That cover up her neck."

"You throw your weight around here.
You think that you're the boss.
You make me tear my hair out.
You really make me cross."

"Oh I know I shouldn't have mentioned 'cross'
It only makes you sore.

But there's no need to get dramatic
And disintegrate on the floor."

"The next time you stay out at night
And flap home here at four,
There will be a sprig of garlic
Hung on every bloody door."

"And I'm fed up with my coffin,
You know my back's not grand,
And those people next door, the Werewolves
Have got a slumberland."

"I don't think that I ask for much
It's not as if I'm proud.
But don't you think it's time I had
At least another shroud."

"You used to be young and handsome
When years ago, we wed,
But now I look at your false fangs
In the glass beside my bed."

"Oh I've had offers from other men,
Men so proud and fine.
Only the other day I was asked
To dine with Frankenstein."

"And what about all these virgins?
There's a new one on the rack.
I'm the one who has to dispose
Of all those bodies out the back."

"I've even gone to the hospital,
Withdrawn blood from the hospital bank,
So when you haven't got enough,

It's me you have to thank."

"Oh please, dear wife," said Dracula,
"Don't nag me so, I'm tired,
Tonight down in the churchyard
Left a great deal to be desired."

"Just get my slippers and give me a chair,
I'll just rest in my den.
What is to eat? I hope it's good.
Oh God, not stake again."

1 Retirement

So my husband and I have retired
and it's true I'm making my plans.
I don't want to be bored
so we could go abroad
and then we can top up our tans.

I told him that we could go shopping
for shorts and bikinis and trews.
But he just said "WHAT?"
cos he'd rather not
and he didn't welcome my news.

I want to wear leathers,
and dance using feathers,
and kick up my heels at the moon
for this life is mine
and I like my glass of wine.
Will all be finished too soon?

He lies on the couch, and he doesn't speak.
He lies there not making a sound.
He watches Dad's Army, and Del Boy, and such,
the second and third time around.

While I want to do belly dancing
with a bra and some knickers to match.
With big silver earrings and big silver sequins
all stuck on my HRT patch.

I had notions of retiring together
and going quite mad every day.
But I'm here on the couch
with this lazy louch,
and my life is just slipping away.

2 Carousel

In a dark deserted town
In depths of winter,
Feeling very down
I looked for life
Which every town in winter lacks.

I heard a sound
That stopped me in my tracks.
Fairground music played
Eerily into the night.

I followed it until there came into my sight
A carousel tucked behind the harbour wall,
and there an old man leaning on a stall.

"Do you want a ride?" and beckoned me,
I said Yes.
It was impulsive.
I climbed the steps
and chose my steed and started off
at gentle speed.

My horse was black with silver prancing feet,
He seemed alive,
I swear I felt his heat.
Round and round and on and on I soared,
While rain lashed down and wind around me roared.

Then slowly quietly did it slow and run.
I turned to thank the man for all the fun.

I went back there and looked the following day
But all was quiet in that deserted bay.
I asked a man about the eerie carousel.

He said, "Old Sam is dead and gone to Hell.
He has been dead these forty years my dear".

"He fell and drowned just off the North shore pier.
They say if you stop and ride his carousel,
You too will drown and go to Hell".

He walked away and I could only stare
And listen to the music hanging in the air,
And soon I knew I'd feel the ghostly horse's breath,
And ride the carousel to certain death.

3 Bill's Demise

When Molly's husband upped and died
Molly sighed and Molly cried.
But what the neighbours didn't know
Is that it was simply done for show.

For Molly wasn't sad at all
And here's a thing that will appal.
Molly was relieved and glad.
How could she be distressed and sad.

When his demise was her release,
For now, at last a bit of peace.
How blissful now to dine alone.
The double bed would be her own.

And she could come and go at will
Without a questionnaire from Bill.
Oh she would never want him back,
But at the graveside she wore black.

And cried and cried and hid her guile
And emulated crocodile.
But then when all had left the grave
And called her steadfast, strong and brave,
She took the car and then did park it
Outside the nearest supermarket.

And filled the trolley to the brim
With stuff she never bought with him
Chocolates, cake, and lots of wine
Thinking, all of this is minc.

When she got home, she filled a cup
And turned the central heating up.
So when you see a widow crying
Remember, she could well be lying.

4 Appropriate Clothes

I'm lying in the hospital
Feeling rather ill,
Having had bronchitis,
I've rather had my fill.

An ambulance has rushed me in.
I had no chance to pack.
And here I am with not much on,
Lying on my back.

So, husband has been visiting,
And I told him what to do.
I need nighty, soap, and dressing gown,
I needed knickers too.

I gave him just a little list,
But it gave him quite a pause.
He didn't know where nighties were,
Let alone my drawers.

He doesn't go in cupboards
To see where things are kept,
And as for doing household things
He is really quite inept.

Oh, he knows where the remote control is.
He knows about TV.
But he doesn't know where clothes are kept,
Especially for me.

He cannot put a wash on.
He cannot cook a dinner.
By the time that I get out of here
He should be two stone thinner.

It's been some time and I am well,
It's time to pack my case,
Comb my hair and brush my teeth,
Put make up on my face.

He is bringing me a dress in,
I told him where to look.
It's in the larger wardrobe
Hanging on a hook.

So, I leave the ward and as I go
I see the nurses frown.
I'm the only lady going home
In a low-cut sparkly evening gown.

5 Drink

I'm fed up today, pass the brandy.
I've just lost my way, pass the port.
My moods are erratic, I'm less than ecstatic.
I'm even more sad than I thought.

My life is a mess, pass the vodka.
And nothing looks good, pass the gin.
It's the only way I can cope with today.
I wish that my life would begin.

I am feeling so bad, pass the whisky.
I am feeling so sad, pass the rum.
I am here all alone and my heart is like stone.
I am sad and I'm drunk and I'm glum.

I am filling my glass with Bacardi.
I am opening a bottle of wine.
My head feels so thick, and I want to be sick.
I am putting myself on the line.

I am tapping a barrel of beer.
One barrel should be enough.
And when I dive in, I won't try to swim.
I'll just give up and drown in the stuff.

6 Get a Life

"Get a life Courtnay,"
Her mother snarled.
"I'm sick of hearing you whine.
Get a life Courtnay,
Why don't you grow up?
Get a personality like mine."

"Don't you like my new boyfriend
With the rings in his nose?
Don't you like all his nice tattoos?
I know he can be funny,
And nasty sometimes,
When high on the pills and the booze".

"Get a life Courtnay.
Why don't you grow up?
I do all I can for your sake."

"I buy you new videos and burgers and chips.
Why don't you just give me a break?"

And the four-year-old sighed,
And sucked at her thumb,
And knew that she wasn't ready,
To become like her mother, or boyfriend or both,
As she walked away with her teddy.

7 Declutter

I went to a seminar about living and life
And how to beat failure and stress.
I'd been feeling quite low for ages it seems,
At my age I felt quite a mess.

The lady stood up and said, "Listen to me,
Start by throwing things out of the house."
But could I part with my books, could I part with my clothes,
Could I part with the small china mouse?

"De clutter," she said, "Get rid of the stuff,
Get shot of all you don't need."
So I thought, and I realised how she was right,
And I flew home with gusto and speed.

I looked at my all, and thought what don't I need?
What is the thing to get rid.
Then I suddenly knew what vexed me the most,
So I threw out the husband and kid.

8 Thomas Dodge

Thomas Dodge was on manoeuvres
with his rough-hewn army mates,
when he came upon an old sheep
slumped against the old farm gates.

She had been dying since come sun up,
every breath seemed like her last.
Thomas Dodge he stopped and saw her,
looked at her with eyes aghast.

Clouds of flies had settled on her
when she inhaled she breathed them in,
then out again and gasped and panted.
Thomas Dodge thought this a sin.

Thomas Dodge had been a farmer
before the time he went to war.
He stood before the sheep a'dying,
he was appalled by what he saw.

He took his rifle and he pointed
though the act filled him with dread,
closed his eyes and pulled the trigger,
shot the sheep right through her head.

Thomas Dodge was reprimanded,
made to justify what he'd done.
They said he wasted ammunition,
said he had misused his gun.

But his Captain was a man of honour,
said that Thomas Dodge was right.
Would like him near him in a battle,
would like him near him in a fight.

Said that Dodge had had compassion,
as you sew so shall you reap.
Thomas Dodge was then promoted
Giving mercy to a sheep.

9 Life's Like That

The birds are singing in Park Street
And blossom hangs over old grey walls.
But down in Coronation Road
The dust gets in your eyes,
And old dogs lie on broken doorsteps
Heaving sighs.

The sun is shining in Park Street
The grass is green
And the windows gleam,
But down in Coronation Road
The sky is grey
And people will not stop
To pass the time of day.

Children run laughing in Park Street
To ballet lessons in pink ribboned shoes.
But down in Coronation Road
The children fight, over broken gateposts
In the fading light.

And I once lived in Park Street
'Til me husband died,
And my children cried.
But now I live in Coronation Road
In a two-room flat,
And my children ask, "Why is that?"
And I say,
"Why! Life's like that."

10 What's in a Name?

I want my name to be ZaSu Pitts,
Not plain old Janice Price.
I don't want a name that's meek and mild
Or one that's boring and nice.

I want my name to be Tallulah Bankhead,
Or something equally crazy.
Not Jane nor June nor Janice,
Not Anne nor Betty nor Daisy.

If they ask you, "Who's important?"
You can stand up and say, "I am,"
With a name like Isambard Kingdom Brunel,
Or the title of Omar Khayyam.

You have to amount to something
If your name is Robespierre,
Or Leonardo da Vinci,
You have to be something rare.

So, bear with me while I change my name,
That my flamboyant lifestyle befits.
And even when I'm eighty
And I'm drunk and doing the splits.

Or when I'm in the Bowls Club
With Danny in his Panama hat,
It won't matter if I'm silly
Or over made up and fat.

I'll have had a really fantastic life
Living on my wits,
And they'll say, "Oh she's a character
For her name is ZaSu Pitts."

11 Brightness

Yesterday morning I woke early,
The whole day was filled with promise and love.
My white dress hung, shining bright,
Outside, the sun was brightly shining.

The orange blossom wreath was there
For my brushed and brightly shining hair.
Something borrowed, something blue was there.
Pearls were scattered and little flowers
Filling the room with their perfume.

I shall always hate roses,
I shall always hate white,
And bright mornings,
And Bells.

12   The Stone Cat

There is a little stone cat on a wall
There is Ivy growing like a crown of green
Around his stony brow.

He sits for all eternity
Moss grows between his toes.

Who made him?
The man who built the wall?
Was he proud of his wall,
And added the cat as a flourish?

Or did he get tired of putting stone upon stone
And added the cat in defiance?
How long has he been sitting, the cat?
A long time I would say.

He watches mice and birds with longing eyes
And cannot flex a claw
He seems to care
He cannot rip and tear
Who put him there?

13 The Glutton

Mary, Rosina, Evangeline, Jane,
you have been in the pantry
again and again.

You have been at the ham,
you have been at the jelly.
You're large in the chest
and rotund in the belly.

Your ankles are thick
and your two chins are wobbling.
Why don't you stop
your continual gobbling.

No one will love you if you get very fat.
You are quite a ridiculous size
for a cat.

14 Your Particular Death

I hear the juke box play my love
As I gaze into your empty eyes.
I bought you a rose of red and white
To counteract your lies.

We went to the cinema nightly, my love
But the blood just made you sick.
You cried when you saw the soldier's grave
Marked with a twisted stick.

You went in the garden and stole me a frog
You did your best to convince
That if I kissed it long enough
It would become a handsome prince.

I kissed it every day for a year
Under a waiting sky.
But there in the cold cathedral
It became a hover fly.

The cat's claws hide in velvet my love
And the devil hides in me
I hear the juke box play my love
But your eyes no longer see.

15 Feeling Low

If I'm feeling very low,

I paint, and draw, and knit, and sew,

and if I'm feeling worse than that,

I drink and throw up on the mat.

16 The Right

I plant cabbages for slugs to feast on,

I help spiders out of the bath.

I carry woodlice out to the garden,

I move snails off the road,

And then worry if they are lost.

So called normal people

Think I am a little mad,

I think they are totally insane.

I think everything has a right to life.

17 Anne the Arsonist

Please may I have your attention,
I've a story to relate,
About a girl who hated men,
And viscous was her hate.

They called her Anne the Arsonist,
And I'm really not a liar.
When I say with all authority,
She set everything on fire.

I wouldn't say she was crazy,
But she was verging on the brink.
Her handbag was a gasoline can.
She was dressed in paraffin pink.

Her dress was silk and sexy,
The colour of a flame.
Things would hot up really fast,
But she was not to blame.

She was the illegitimate daughter of a fireman,
And had never seen her dad,
So she kept on lighting fires.
Some of them were really bad.

Then she would scrutinise each fireman
Wondering if it were he
Who had loved her mam and left them.
No one hated more than she.

She set fire to endless pubs and clubs.
It was wrong, what can you say.
She was a scourge in every village.
There was a fire every day.

She set fire to bingo halls as well.
She caused a lot of deaths.
Poor sweet Anne the Arsonist
With her matches and her meths.

She loved the 5th of November,
It was her favourite night,
With her pockets full of fireworks,
She would set the town alight.

She didn't have much luck with men
Whatever shape or size,
For she had to set them all on fire
'Tis true I tell no lies.

They avoided her at all times
When she was near, they'd cringe
For they knew that Anne the Arsonist
Would make them char and singe.

You could always tell where Anne walked
As furious flames grew higher.
She set fire to the local school,
And danced around the funeral pyre.

The local firemen loved our Anne
They didn't mind her crime
For she kept them busy all the day
With lots of overtime.

One time she found a boyfriend,
And even thought of marriage
She loved his occupation
He was the owner of a garage.

She loved him for a lot of things.

Her love was very keen.
She loved his five-star petrol
And his cans of gasoline.

She was a favourite with the extremists
When to North Wales she did roam.
She had a lovely full-time job
Setting fire to the holiday home.

She finally met her match one day
A man so sure to beat her.
She tried to set this chap alight
But he was a fire-eater.

He followed her around the town
She'd plan a fire and set it,
But found it came to nothing
Because her boyfriend always ate it.

And now she rarely thinks of him.
It was one of her bad phases,
And in the end she told him
That he could go to blazes.

And if you meet Anne the Arsonist
And ask of her his name
"Oh him," she'll say, "I can't remember
He's only my old flame."

18 Llangynwyd

Christmas night when stars are shining
And the robin's voice is still,
I seem to hear Llangynwyd calling
From my cottage on the hill.

And the welcome from the Tylers Arms
Brings a tear to my eye,
And makes me long for my Llynfi Vale.
To return before I die.

Good friends mean all the world to me
And songs to touch my heart.
I pray this place will never change
For it is a world apart.

So thank God for the singing,
For that happiness I yearn.
Make sure this place will stay the same
Until I can return.

19 Bus Stop Thoughts, Scribbled on a Cheque Book.

I was standing at the bus stop
In poetry mode
When Bedlington and man
Came down the road.

The dog he looked at me
With weary eyes
His master never looked
I tell no lies.

They passed and I waited
For the bus.
I stood there
With a minimum of fuss.

While I just stood there looking
And wondering why
A buzzard flew an arc
Across the sky.

The catkins hung their heads
Across the wall
And I could make no sense
Of life at all.

I wrote a poem,
I just scribbled in poetry mode
When Bedlington and man
Came down the road.

I signed the poem and my gladness
Knew no bounds.
The bank, they cashed it
For one hundred pounds.

20 The Undertaker's Apprentice

Paul Collins
Wanted to be an undertaker.
All his boyhood life he dreamed of it,
While waiting for destiny,
To fulfil his dream,
He went on a government training scheme.

They sent him to a local Cash and Carry,
And as he walked amongst the shelves,
Of jam and beans.
Longing came over him in waves.

To be amongst.
Grey, granite, graves,
He knew he'd have to change his name.
To something noble
With a distinctive ring
So he could dignity to the profession bring.

He wondered if it would be too pushing
If he changed his name to Peter Cushing?

He helped to lay his Granny out
And his Uncle Len.
He hadn't enjoyed himself so much,
Since he didn't know when!

He laid out his Aunts,
Mary and Bertha.
And he became famous,
All over Merthyr.

People would send for our Paul saying,
"Quick, Grandad's died.

And we don't know what to do."
And Paul would come.
Black of tie,
Black of hat.
And black of shoe!

If for some reason of bodies, there was no surplus.
Paul would kill,
his unfortunate pets,
On purpose!

People in Merthyr became afraid to be ill,
For Paul could hardly wait,
For an empty grave to fill.

His Mother kept on crying.
And thought of Paul.
And put off dying!

His Dad, thought him completely mad.
And tried to talk him into joining up.
But Paul rebelled.
And said he wasn't barmy,
And preferred undertaking to any army!

His Father fumed.
And had a heart attack.
And Paul was there.
Ready.
All in black!

He went to see the local undertaker.
And asked to become an apprentice.
He looked Paul over and asked.
"Do you like this place?"
And noted the satisfied smile,

That lit our little teenager's face!

And now Paul's troubled spirit is so calm.
He's learned to inject.
And stuff.
And embalm.

Paul goes about his work very proud.
Handling hearse and coffin,
Corpse and shroud.

He strides through Merthyr,
With his coat tails flapping.
His silver headed cane,
tapping, tapping.

He has become the happiest man in town.
Weighing people up.
And,
Putting people down!

21 An Epitaph

A Magpie came.
He flew to rest upon my tree.
And knowing him,
he put the fear of God in me.

His plumage sleek,
this evil bird with baleful eye
had visited me once before and watched me die.
As you walked away from me in an empty wood
after telling me that our love never could
survive this thoughtless cruel world.

As Magpie preened, and carefully each feather twirled,
'Tis no wonder that I hate thee wretched bird,
for you were witness when he spoke the word
And now I feel you come to gloat,
and I am weak.

Come, steal the shiny tear upon my cheek.
And take it to your nest above,
And let it be an epitaph to love.

22 I Remember the Wood

I remember the wood

And your dear face.

The mushrooms, and bluebells,

And spider lace.

The evening chorus.

The moon's soft light.

Primrose, anemone,

And owls in flight.

I remember the wood

And your dear face.

How in love we were,

And our state of grace.

When snow and ice,

And nothing mattered.

That's where I want my ashes scattered.

23 The Lonely Place

She was in the house all day alone.
She rarely used the door, or phone.
Waiting for the husband's key
No one loved him more than she.

Yet when he came, he spoke no word,
None that she had ever heard.
He punched the TV button, then
He walked into his private den.

She made him dinner every night,
And in between each careful bite,
He didn't even look at her.
But that was just the way they were.

And as he lifted knife and fork
She longed for him to look, and talk.
And ask about her boring day
But he had nothing left to say.

And even not one word was said
When he fumbled in the marriage bed

She felt as used as any whore,
As she lay there, and he did snore.

She thought to scream once, very loud,
But knew that she was far too proud.
She often thought of using violence
To end that dreadful, endless, silence.

She wondered what would people think
If she walked out, when he didn't drink?
He didn't beat her, keep her short
They never, ever, ever, fought.

Would she be justified to walk,
Just because he didn't talk?
And as tears shone upon her face
She said, - "Marriage is a lonely place."

24 Decorum

Girls you don't need to be naked
To secure the man you adore.
If you cover the things that he craves for
I know he'll be back, that's for sure.

Long ago the flash of an ankle
Would make a man shiver and shake,
And the sight of a knee or a garter
Would certainly keep him awake.

So girls, on the first date say thank you.
And leave him with simply a kiss,
And when he starts getting familiar,
Just tell him you'll give it a miss.

Men always want what they can't have,
So learn how to modestly flirt.
There's no need for the showing of navels.
No need for the miniscule skirt.

Use subtlety, modesty, artistry.
Don't show all your wares at one time,
And he will come crawling I promise,
And a little, will keep him sublime.

When in fancy dress be a Victorian girl,
It's better than cheap plastic nurse,
And leave the French maids there in the shop
Or your image will only get worse.

To fumble in petticoats is every man's dream.
Unlacing bodices too.
He will get quite excited by nothing at all,
Even the turn of a well pointed shoe.

I'm afraid that equality was always a game,
We are up against the proverbial wall.
But if a girl's clever and knows what she's at,
My dears, **you can have it all.**

He will like it if you act like a lady
Although he will never admit.
He would rather you modest and dressed nice
Than itching to get off your kit!

So girls remember, no swearing
Just pleasant and sexy and nice,
And all men will want you I promise
If you take this old experts advice.

25 The Lady

"My kingdom is yonder," she said,
"Just there where the fir trees stand tall.
I have ruled in my castle a very long time.
Just how long I cannot recall."

"Let's ride there this minute." she said.
"The way is both narrow and steep.
We will sit and drink wine, and afterwards dine.
I will show you the lake and the keep."

So I followed her up through the trees,
As I went, was I sealing my fate?
We came to a clearing out of the mist
and entered the large castle gate.

Servants attended our steeds.
I bathed and I dressed in my room
Then I entered the large banquet hall
And walked to a chair in the gloom.

She sat at the head on a throne.
Her gown was encrusted in gold.
She gave the impression of youth,
Although all her companions were old.

We sat and we laughed and drank wine
In that magical place in the mist.
I was only aware of her face,
And the touch of her hand on my wrist.

Then she led me upstairs to her room.
"I will love you forever," she said.
She took off her slippers and gown
And draped herself over the bed.
We made love all through the night,
And I slept like a man who was dead.
As the dawn crept through the casement,

I felt a strange hand on my head.

I awoke with a start, and I saw
The most horrible sight to be seen.
The ugliest crone lay at my side,
Where once the Lady had been.

She was haggard and wrinkled and grey,
Her hand like a claw on my wrist.
Was this my night-time companion?
Was this the thing I had kissed?

She opened her eyes and she cackled
And lifted her arms to my face.
She came at me pulling and clawing.
I could not endure her embrace.

I fled down the stairs full of horror,
Past ruins of stone upon stone.
The servants I'd seen the last evening
Were lying there, bone upon bone.

I ran 'oer the weed covered courtyard,
Praying that it was a dream.
Then high from the old castle turret
Came a terrible blood curdling scream.

I galloped for miles through the woodland
Thrashing my way through the fern
Ne'er looking back the way I had come
Vowing I would never return.

I have heard many tales from old minstrels.
Dark tales of terrible days.
Of a Lady one meets in the woodland,
"My kingdom is yonder," she says.

26 Tradesman

Nothing works in our old place,
It's all a mess, this is the case.
We have no lights with which to see,
And I must say it vexes me.

My Hoover doesn't pick up dust.
The washing machine's beginning to rust.
The iron doesn't work at all,
And sockets hang from off the wall.

I say to my husband, please take stock,
Do you want me to have an electric shock?
The electric fire it burns no more,,
It's no good buying at Curry's store.

For in our house things soon break down.
My husband stands there with a frown.
I've asked him time and again to risk it,
At least the oven, could he fix it?

As long as I'm with this bright spark,
I will always fumble in the dark.
He says, it's all in bad condition,
For my husband is an electrician.

27   Jealousy

My mother loves our old black cat.
She loves it more than me.
She strokes him often, every day
While he sits upon her knee.

He is black and rather scrawny,
A mangy looking bod.
His name is Ozymandias,
Named for an Egyptian God.

I wish I could grow whiskers
And wear a coat of fur,
And when my Mother stroked me,
I'd stretch and loudly purr.

I wish I had his big green eyes
And his awful nightly wail.
I wish I had his pointy ears.
I wish I had his tail.

He shares my Mother's great big bed
And then my Dad gets cross.

And threatens to go elsewhere,
But she doesn't give a toss.

That cat, it rules our tiny house.
It's spoilt beyond compare.
And if it died tomorrow,
I really wouldn't care.

I'd build him a great pyramid
At the bottom of our plot.
Wrap him up in bandages,
Put his innards in a pot.
I know Dad would be thrilled to bits
To see Ozymandias dead.
I'd have my Mother back again,
And Dad would have his bed.

But we are both scared to do it.
We are a pair of fools.
So, in our little terraced house,
Ozymandias rules.

28 Satnav

I bought the gift for Christmas,
It came in a fancy box.
I thought my spouse would like it
Instead of the usual socks.

It was a clever satnav
to put on the dash of his car.
We travel quite a lot you see,
We travel near and far.

The first time that he used it
It told him to turn right.
"Ridiculous," said my husband.
His face was quite a sight.

So, he goes left, and soon the voice
Is saying, "Please turn round."
My husband says it's crazy,
And he makes a snorting sound.

He argues with it daily,
And is even known to shout.

And if I interfere,
He will go into a pout.

The satnav says, "Now you go left."
My husband shouts out, "No."
I realise now it's pointless,
You can't tell this man where to go.

So, when we are in his well-used car
And a route my husband's seeking,
He doesn't like the satnav,
'cos it's a woman that is speaking.
So next Christmas what he's getting
Now the satnav's in its box
Is the same old thing beneath the tree
Two pairs of bloody socks.

29 The Birthday Rose

I took the path that led to the church
Hurrying in the fading light.
I climbed the wall that was near your grave
It would have been your Birthday night.

Tenderly I laid the flower down
On the soft dug mound of earth.
My heart was full of aching love
Devoid of joy and mirth.

I sank in sorrow to the dampening ground
The air was getting colder
And then I felt the gentle touch
Upon my trembling shoulder.

I looked and saw the ruby ring
In the moonlight flashing red
And my heavy heart was filled with pain
And fear and awesome dread.

That dear hand picked up the rose
The rose that I had dropped.
I smelled the scented flower
And it seemed that time had stopped.

I saw your name fresh hewn and raw
Cut in the granite stone
And yet that hand was touching me
A touch I'd always known.

From in the church there came a sound
It was a breath of hymns.
A heavy sweetness came 'oer me
And weighted down my limbs.

But when I turned the hand was gone
And heaven only knows.
You took the gift I'd brought for you
That blood red Birthday Rose.

30 Greenpeace

Look at me.
Said the dog.
On the clean plastic table.
Hear my plea.
I cannot speak out loud.
For they have cut my vocal cords.

Look at me said the rabbit.
In the cage.
My head is fast.
My eyes burn,
For I have been sprayed with hair spray.
Is she or isn't she wearing hair spray?

Look at me said the cat.
Oh, hear me too.
There are wires in my head.
And my children are gone.

What of me said the seal.
They call it a cull.

Look at me said the whale.
Eight out of ten owners say their cats prefer it.

Electric shocks said the monkey.
Are my way of life.
Welcome to Auschwitz.
Welcome to Buchenwald.

Look at me said the lamb.
On a bright springing day.
Lamb for Easter.
With mint sauce of course.

31 A Man of the Cloth

"Oh, I am a high and exalted person.
Kneel all ye before me.
Buy me drinks in the pub.
Stop your foul conversation when I am near."

"For I am a privileged wearer of the cloth.
I am God's messenger.
And my particular message is wrapped
In trendy coloured ribbons."

"I love to be seen running in my cassock.
I speed in my car.
Prepare to meet thy doom.
If I knock you down, I can give you the last rites."

"He's a hell of a character," they say,
"That new vicar."
"I sit writing my sermons stroking my cats.
They mewl for milk, and I caress their fur."

"Young girls adore me,
Old matrons drool over me.
I go into a pub, my scarf around my collar.
A pint of JC please."

"Oh yes, I have those initials on my brain.
My father was a canon
You could say I was the son of a gun
Oh, I can't get any sicker for I am a trendy vicar."

32 Empath

You don't want to be an empath
Just like me.
I smell the passing flower,
I talk to every tree.

I feel the pain in people
when ill or sick at heart.
I even bare my bosom
when they hurl the poison dart.

I hear the scream of every fish
when it's yanked from out the water.
I hear the lambs and heifers
when they take them to the slaughter.

I am a great big golden bowl
which is always brimming over.
I hear the clash of planets
and exploding supernova.

Even atmosphere affects me,
I always soak it in,
and if it's full of hatred
then really, I can't win.

I cannot bear the cruelty
to animal or child.
I can't stand people crying
when their hurt or maimed, defiled.

I feel the pain of orphans
and the loss of widows too.
You take the pain inside your heart
and there's nothing you can do.

I cannot bear the war zones
of shot and shell and bomb.
I cannot watch those war time films
of Passchendaele and Somme.

I am crying for the mother
who lost her precious son.
I am crying for the loser
who a battle never won.

I am crying for the ill ones
who spend their life in pain.
I am crying for the cripple
the elderly and lame.

You don't want to be an empath
to give the people voice
but if you are, it's tough I know,
for you haven't got a choice.

33 Lost World

My grandmother would have apoplexy
If she came back today,
For her world such as it was,
Is changed in every way.

She would not like the television
With its awful reality shows.
And what she'd make of the cinema
Goodness only knows.

She would view the recent fashions
With total abject horror,
And cities partying at night
She'd think Sodom and Gomorrah.

My gran would just be horrified
To see the children not the same.
They are not meek, and the way they speak
Would put a navvy to shame.

I'm afraid she would give them a damn good smack.
You would hear them scream and wail.
And then my poor granny
Would do a stint in jail.

But I think her world was better.
It had everything we lack.
But what's the point of wishing,
You never can go back.

34 Abyss

It's as if you never were,
Except for some intrusive memory
That flickers in and out.
Images of trees and blossom,
hot sun sharp frosts.

Was it so long ago? A different age
When we were young and eager.
To try and find you now
I have to search the troubled sky
The lonely forests
But why would I,
When all it brings is pain?

I am here to be found.
My name is in the phone book.
My spirit is in the needle dark pine
Waiting.

Just don't die on me,
I could not bear that.
I would have to visit your grave
All the time
Prostrate myself weeping.

So keep going,
At least until my heart withers
And shrinks,
And cares no more,
And feels no pain.
Until then I will wander the country lane.
And hope to meet you.

35 If You Could See Me Now

If you could see me now
you would have a shock.
Gucci bag, designer frock.

Long, long ago you'd look and frown
and always, always put me down.
You told me I was dull and slow
and I'd reply, "You never know."

And sure enough, I'm clever, wealthy,
Pretty, prosperous and healthy.
You said I'd never amount to much,
but you are old and out of touch,
and I'm the one who has it all,
with head held high and walking tall,
and you dear Aunt, so full of hate
should never underestimate.

I have done well, you might allow.
If only you could see me now.
But for all my confidence this day,
you still, in your malicious way,
know exactly how to frown
and say the words to put me down,
and I become the child again,
hurting, smarting, full of pain.

But I will win, and this I vow,
and hope you come to see me now.

36 Betty From Bettws and the Great Secret

One day while walking through Maesteg town
I saw an old man get knocked down.
I rushed to his aid, and I heard him mutter
As he lay there dying in the gutter.

He gasped out a tale that was hard to believe.
His bony hand clutched at my sleeve.
He said it all began in 1910
When a woman entered the world of men.

He begged me to tell every Mrs and Mr
The incredible tale of his only sister,
and as I listened there on bended knee,
I will tell you the tale as he told it to me.

His sister's name was Betty.
She was different from the others,
'cos she was the only sister
In a family of brothers.

Their dad had wanted a rugby team,
and I will never forget the morn
he paced up and down at the bottom of the stairs
As his fifteenth child was born.

When the midwife shouted "It's a girl"
His aged heart it sunk
and he went down to The Oddfellows Arms
and got raging, stinking drunk.

When he got home and looked at his boys
he cried just like the rain.
Put on his Dai cap, went out the door
and was never seen again.

Four months later, Betty's Mum
was playing bingo in the hall.

She only needed 37
To win that night's snowball.

Thirty six was called and thirty five,
and finally thirty four,
and when thirty seven was finally called,
Her Mum was on the floor.

The excitement was too much for her,
And after much proddings and pokes
they realised she was really dead,
and Betty had no folks.

So Betty's brothers brought her up
though she lacked a little poise.
By the time our girl was 18 years old
the girl was one of the boys.

They handed down each rugby shirt.
They handed down their socks.
They taught young Betty to play good darts.
They taught her how to box.

Then her elder brother went on a trip
to an old boys' darts re-union.
There were thirty of them going
and they went to the Soviet Union.

There he met a Russian girl
and she was quite well known.
She was the Russian top shot putter
and weighed in at nineteen stone.

She'd been on anabolic steroids
which made her grow and tower,
building mighty muscles
and giving her much power.

So he brought some home for Betty

Who thought that they were sweets
and took the tablets every day
and performed amazing feats.

She began to put on size and weight,
A change came in her figure.
Her chest expanded every day,
Everything grew bigger.

Every day she watched her brothers
Play their rugby game,
Until one day her brother Will
got kicked and went home lame.

So Betty took his place at once
they were playing against Tondu,
and after forty minutes
they were winning nineteen three.

Now the big five happened to be watching
that day in Maesteg town.
They could see our Bet's potential
they could see the triple crown.

Betty's brothers were proud of her
the way she swerved and ran.
They didn't tell the selectors
that Bet was not a man.

Her brothers knew when Betty
was finally full grown.
She could have tackled Pontypool front row
Completely on her own.

No one guessed the secret
only Betty's brothers,
and they whisked her away from every game
So as not to show the others.

Some thought that it was funny
the way her shorts did fit,
and a couple of things they noticed
Like, no jock strap in her kit.

The way she was so tidy,
and always cleaned her daps.
Knitted all her rugby socks,
stitched lace upon her caps.

One day she beat a player up
for he had made it known
that Betty, in the changing rooms
was reading 'Woman's Own'.

But one day while in the showers
a boy I will not name
discovered Betty's secret
he said, "She's not the same."

But the Welsh selectors watched her
and noticed Betty's skills.
They didn't know about the secret
nor the anabolic pills.

They were on the look-out for talent
in rugby playing males,
and Betty went on trial
to play the game for Wales.

The game was the best one ever
and Betty made her mark.
It was a woman's greatest triumph
at Cardiff Arms Park.

Max Boyce wrote a song for her,
you know he's got the cheek.
But Bet, she had him by the scruff
And made him eat his leek.

They played against the English,
A team of some renown.
Bet was biggest in the line up
she always tapped it down.

She played the game tremendously
and finally won the day,
with the greatest ever touch down
from thirty yards away.

She waded through the Englishmen
using her great bulk.
She was like a moving mountain
or a stand in for the hulk.

After the game she was whisked away
to her private showers,
and there her brothers toasted her
with Brains Dark and gave her flowers.

Then through the door there came a man
his Dai cap in his hand.
His beard it was three foot long,
his face was lean and tanned.
Betty cried. "Who is this man?
He shouldn't be in here"
then Betty noticed her brothers,
in every eye a tear.

It's Dad they shouted gleefully.
He has come from far away.
"Do tell us Dad, did you watch the game,
Did you see Betty play?"

"I've travelled all the world," said he,
"I've just myself to blame,
but I'm proud today of being Welsh
after seeing Betty's game."

Then he collapsed and fell to the ground
For he was in bad condition.
But he died that day with a smile on his face
Fulfilling his life's ambition.

But something happened after that,
our Bet went to a dance,
and had to make a rapid choice,
Rugby or romance.

Her disappearance has remained
A mystery unsolved.
Although the rumours they were rife
and round the Town revolved.

So in my arms the old man died,
The last of Betty's brothers,
and I've tried to tell the secret
to many many others.

But when I relate the story
to an audience of only males,
They will never, ever accept the fact.
THAT A WOMAN PLAYED FOR WALES.

37   Cowboy Ballad

His horse galloped on
Through the desert and plain.
He had ridden for days,
He was riddled with pain.

Across his broad saddle
He carried a dress.
Beautiful silk,
For his glorious Bess.

Covered in frills
Of Chantilly Lace.
A gossamer veil
To cover her face.

He would marry his woman
In the old Spanish town.
He imagined his Bess
In the glorious gown.

He rode into town
At sunrise that morn,
Tired and thirsty
And ragged and worn.

He went into the bar,
The whole room went still.
They knew when they told him
He'd be looking to kill.

For Bess had not waited,
She now had another,
And somebody told him
She now loved his brother.

He stormed from the room
And went to find Bess.
He cursed her and hit her
And made her confess.

He told her to strip
At the point of a gun.
He could not believe
What his brother had done.

He cursed her and told her
To put on the dress,
Then shot her and killed
His beautiful Bess.

And he roared to the heavens
And cursed all his kin,
Turned the gun on himself,
Now no one would win.

His brother came then
To the dead and the dying.
Saw the result
Of his cheating and lying.

Buried them both
And there they both lay,
To wander as ghosts
To this very day.

A broken young cowboy
And his lover Bess,
Walking the plain
In her white wedding dress.

38 Old Grey Walls

Old grey walls in sad decay
crumbling away,
once they stood fine and proud
in rolling hills of green.

Flags flew from proud monuments,
gay and bright.
Battles raged around your walls,
fierce and blazing.

Dancers pivoted within,
swirling, swaying.
Sad to see you falling, left to die.
Old grey walls
beneath an old grey sky.

39 The Pub Landlady. With a nod to John Betjeman's 'Sun and Fun' poem.

I walked into the bar one rainy morning
There were fag ends lying stamped into the floor
There was something that was squashed
And the glasses were unwashed
There was chewing gum on the handle of the door.

I pulled aside the crimson velvet curtains
I used to think them classy but they're not
The sunshine tried to shine
On the dregs of the curdled wine
And I knew I was unhappy with my lot.

I owed the brewery lots and lots of money
They threatened to stop the dray the following week
There's the tax and there's the VAT
All the bills are on the mat
Where can I find the help that I must seek?

I caught sight of my reflection in the mirror
Of the girl that I once was there, is no trace
It's true my looks are going
My black roots are darkly showing
And the lines are marching square across my face.

It's no wonder that my husband up and left me
Marriage doesn't thrive when you both drink
It's hard to keep your vows
As the customers watch the rows
As you always end up crying in the sink.

You get up very early to clean the toilets
Someone's taken all the bulbs and toilet roll
So you scrub out all the sinks
And top up all the drinks
And wonder if life's better on the dole.

Men say their wives don't understand them
They have stories and they tell me what is wrong
They can really bore for Wales
While I have loads of tales
But they never let me talk for very long.

I knew I had to open in an hour
I open every night and every day
I wanted gin or brandy
But settled for a shandy
And vowed to find the guts to run away.

And now I know we are a dying breed
When did anyone see a Landlady last?
Counting up the stock
In her cheap and shiny frock
I'm afraid that all the glory days are past.

All the pubs are closing in the town
There are more of them almost every day
Pubs are now for scoffing
And the last nail in the coffin
Was the smoking ban that somehow came to stay.

My customers were old and mostly miners
Who came here for a chat and pint and smoked
And now they stand outside
A fact I can't abide
On the pavement in the cold and getting soaked.

Where will they go when my door finally closes,
And the windows boarded up and it's for sale?
When all the people want is nosh
In a restaurant that's quite posh
Paying three pounds for a pint of watered ale.

If I play a bit of music for a party
I've got to pay for that there is no doubt
There's the bill for heat and lights

And of course performing rights
It makes you wonder what it's all about.

By midnight you are coming to the finish
But they want an extra drink served with a smile
Their faces all are beaming
And you know you will start screaming
Because all you want to do is run a mile.

There were good times in the past I'm not saying
There were parties balls and tastings every week
With my sleek and coiffured tresses
And my shiny satin dresses
I was fabulous and really at my peak.

Now I'm hoovering the beer sodden carpet
Wiping nicotine off the pictures in the hall
I just feel old and spent
And I cannot pay the rent
I am desperate and my back's against the wall.

Down the road they have opened up a Wetherspoons
It's enough to make an honest person weep
It leaves me quite bereft
All my regulars have left
Because their food and beer is so cheap.

Now in comes Tom and the other alcoholics
To share my life of fun and wine and beer
So I summon up a smile
And all the bloody while
I try to hide my misery and fear.

40   The Bequest

All night long he bought me drinks
called me his bit of stuff.
By half past ten I was fed up,
I'd really had enough.

He said, "I want your body
I can never have my fill".
So I said that he could have it,
and left it to him in my will.

41 Nostalgia

When bulls had rings in their noses
And sailors sported tattoos
And navvies were the ones that were swearing
And girls wore white high heeled shoes.

When women never wore trousers
Or cut their hair like a man.
When lying out in the sunshine
Was the way for getting a tan.

When Groucho Marx had the eyebrows
And boxers had lips that were fat,
And nails were polished and shapely,
Not sharp pointy claws like a cat.

When a man from Brazil was Brazilian,
And only the clowns had blue hair.
When fashion was stylish and elegant,
And everybody had flair.

When policemen were totally respected,
And you didn't mind being a nerd.

When teachers were authority figures,
And children were seen and not heard.

When you were stuck with the breasts you were born with,
And teeth were a natural shade.
When we all went to church on a Sunday,
And sang to the Lord and then prayed.

When we all didn't need this new vaccine
To save us from Covid-19.
I remember, oh yes, I remember
All the things I have seen.

When burglars and thieves were the ones in the masks.
When going to the pub was good fun.
When you wouldn't wake up of a morning
To find that your daughter's your son!

That's the time when I was so happy,
When I knew what to say and to wear.
When a man from Brazil was Brazilian
And only the clowns had blue hair.

42 Witness

He said he was a witness
Of the Jehovah kind,
And different books and doctrine
Had blown away his mind.

He was shivering on my doorstep
In the rain and fading light,
So I took his arm and brought him in
At the time I thought it right.

I made him tea and biscuits
As I would for any friend,
And he told me that I must repent
Before the world did end.

He talked of Armageddon
And the end of the human race,
While I observed his slender hands
And drank in his handsome face.

He didn't know my passion
And how deep was my great need.
He promised he would come again
And gave me books to read.

He came again the following week
And again, I asked him in.
I listened to his ranting
While I supped my glass of gin.

He resisted all my offerings
And my attempts to woo.
But he got just what he wanted
Now I'm a witness too.

43 Things Don't Change

The medieval lady smiles,
the centuries are vast,
stretching out and back in years,
she contemplates the past.

The men she loved, the men she knew,
she knew it was the truth,
that medieval men were rough,
rugged, and uncouth.

Their manners were so hard to bear,
they reeked of meat and wine.
They sickened her, disgusted her,
for she was a lady fine.

And the reason for her smiling?
As she watches from her wall,
she realised something obvious,
Men haven't changed at all.

44 Nevermore

Omar Khayyam spent lots of time in gardens
With his loaf of bread and his jug of wine.
But when my moving finger writes
On busy weekday nights
I have to work before I write a line.

Now Edgar Allan Poe was fairly miserable.
He spent his life depressed and down and sore,
But he knew he had a perk
When he didn't have to work.
To work I'd like to say, "Oh nevermore."

Did Kipling ever wash or sweep or dust?
Did Browning ever clean while he took notes?
Did Dylan fetch the coal,
While searching of his soul?

Did Robbie Burns compose while stirring oats?
Wordsworth strolled in peace amid the daffodils.
He wrote poems cos he'd nothing else to do
Just to sup a glass of wine,
And write a clever line.

With time, I'm sure that I could do it too.
Oh I wish I could just sit down by a fountain
And make up lovely rhymes the live long day.
But I have to go and sort out what's for dinner
And then this poet has to earn her pay.

45 Mary

"I wish my husband was dead," said Mary,
"For then I would have much more leisure.
I suppose I could kill him,
With toadstools could fill him.
It would give me the greatest of pleasure."

"And after the funeral," said Mary,
"I would buy a new dress made of lace.
It would have to be black,
With no front and no back,
And I'd fall out all over the place."

"You've heard of the merry widow," said Mary,
"She would look very sad next to me,
In my chastity belt
Made of silver and felt,
And I'd give all my lovers a key."

"I'd have to go to Spain," said Mary,
"To make my sorrow much lighter,
And of course I'd be met
In my need to forget
By an amorous handsome bullfighter."

"It's no use just thinking," said Mary,
I'll go to the woods that are near.
The toadstools I'll fetch
And I'll say to that wretch,
Come eat up your breakfast my dear."

46 Sing Your Song

Hey Mr guitar player, who's been hurting you?
Tell me all about it if you can.

You can lose yourself in music
But you still can't lose the pain.

You can sing some pretty love songs
But you know it's all in vain.

For your life is all but over
And the best things are all gone.

So hey Mr guitar player,
Sing your song.

Hey Mr guitar player, why do you look so down.
Tell me all about it if you can.

All around you is the beauty
But you still don't want to see.

You are crying deep inside you
And your heart just isn't free.

And your life just has no meaning
For the best things are all gone.

So hey Mr guitar player
Sing your song.

47 Stone

The statue stood,
He could do little else.
He was cold with a seeping cold.
There were vague stirrings
Beneath his stony breast.

He was well proportioned,
Carved out of a solid boulder.
The ivy curling around his big toe
Annoyed him greatly.
It was creeping up his leg.

He imagined it twining around his genitals.
The thought made his groin retract
As if he was a real man.
He stood amongst the trees
Petrified for all time.

Once a girl came and ran her fingers
Over the granite grooves of his face.
In winter, snow settled on his brow.
His eyes like cracked glass were blind,

Like small frozen pools.

If he cried it would be like hail
Bouncing down to the earth beneath.
He was alone, trapped inside this sculptural cast.
He could hear the scream of birds
And feel their tiny feet on his shoulders.

He couldn't smell the roses
Nor hear the catkins weeping.
He looked down at the grey clinging grave sod
That surrounded him.

There was no one there but him
And corpses. Dead and frozen corpses.
He was perfect except for one thing
The chip on his shoulder.

48 Bertie

Bertie was a battered husband,
His wife was bigger than him.
He wanted to end his marriage,
But the chances of that were slim.

Everyday his wife beat him
Till he was black and blue.
He was frightened of his shadow,
He didn't know what to do.

He was so much of a weakling,
Knobbly kneed and skinny.
He spent hours in the kitchen
Crying in his pinny.

He wanted to be like other men
And have a life so free,
Instead of spending half his life
Over a woman's knee.

His wife was in the dart team.
He was left alone a lot,
Washing, cleaning, cooking,
Putting baby in her cot.

He knew he could stand this life no more,
It would have to reach its end,
So he swallowed a cup of Harpic
And went completely round the bend.

49 Modern Brides

When first we met a year ago
You loved my eyes and hair.
You told me I looked lovely,
That no one could compare.

We wed upon a glorious day,
The sun shone from above.
You looked so handsome by my side,
We were both in love.

My dress it cost a thousand pounds,
The reception was much more.
But I didn't care, why should I,
As you whisked me round the floor.

As in the posh hotel we danced
And vowed not to forsake
Each other, as we cut
Our three-tier wedding cake.

We have got a house in Legoland
With furniture brand new.
Huge windows, a conservatory
To admire the lovely view.

A kitchen just to die for
With all the latest stuff.
I want it all, I need it all,
I will never have enough.

You never asked if I could cook
Or tidy up a room.
You never questioned my expertise
With duster, mop and broom.

You were glad to kiss me every day
And fondle me by night.
You never asked if I could iron
Or get your best shirt white.

So tell me why you do it now?
Why moan about the dust?
It never bothered you before
When your eyes were on my bust.

Your eyes were only fixed on me,
You said it with a look.
I didn't know when I married you
I would have to clean and cook.

I'm not messing up my kitchen
No matter what you say.
So go and get the car out
And get a take-away.

And if it doesn't suit you
And you look at me with remorse,
Well that's OK I'm fed up too.
We will get a quick divorce.

50 The News

You phoned me up today my friend,
But what you told me on the phone
Was completely unexpected.
The tests are back, you said to me
And I'm afraid from where I'm stood
The doctor put it bluntly,
It wasn't looking good.

He's given me 18 months you said,
Give or take a day.
And then my life is over
And I didn't know what to say.
You seemed to take it calmly.
You sounded positive and sane,
Although you told me on the phone
You'd been on the champagne.

I've drunk all day, you said to me.
I'm trying to keep a hold.
But I kind of went to pieces
After I'd been told.

I'm thinking of going to Malta, you said

I've heard it's very nice.

I know you've been there often.

I'd like some good advice.

So do drop in when you have time,

I'm feeling rather low,

And I'm sorry if I've shocked you,

I just wanted you to know.

I put the phone down and I sat,

I knew I shouldn't weep.

I also knew, my dear friend,

That I will have no sleep.

What can I do to help you?

There must be words to say,

To stop this thing from happening

And make it go away.

51   The Boy

Stupidity pursues you
Like a grey shadow.

You close your eyes
Like a gangling Ostrich
Thrusting your head in the sand.

Weak eyes look out
From a brain in a similar condition.

Poor fool,
Striving and hoping
That all will be well.

Can you ignore the dark beast of knowledge
That yaps at your heels?

You cry at toys snatched away
Out of your unworthy hands.

Like a child you weep
At the taking down of decorations.

You don't live life,

You meander through it,

Lost and unsuccoured.

You are the baby who weeps for his mother's breast,

Which has long dried up and shrivelled.

Your bed is lonely,

With only your hand for company.

And your unprotesting pillow

Lying like an old used up whore at your side.

They do not mate, the wild tempestuous sea

With sickly pallid moon.

She wanders lonely skies,

And as for your dreams,

Why! Stars are wearing them as shrouds.

52 Tears

There is weeping at the pit head today.
Men are Trapped underground.
Dust and silence hang around
Except for the women sobbing.

Dai Jones' mother is crying too,
Into her apron made out of a sack,
Broken like Dai's back.

Dai Jones went down the mine today
In his dada's cast-off boots.
Twelve years old and a smile like the morning.

Mair Richards lost her man today,
Handsome he was and carefree.
They would have been wed in the bright tomorrow.
He carved her a love spoon
With hearts and stars.
To match your eyes, he said.

Now he is dead.
Cradling little Dai to his chest
In the smoke and the dust,
His teeth shining white
By the light of his candle
Before it went out.

53 Running Away

A circus coming to Brecon
And I'm thinking of running away.
It will be in the town
And I could be clown
Or feeding the horses their hay.

I could live in a gay caravan
And tell fortunes a fiver a time.
I could dance round the fire
And learn the high wire
And flirt with the man who does mime.

There's a circus coming to Brecon
And I'm thinking that this is for me.
I'll put on some spangles,
Some earrings and bangles
And eat candy floss for my tea.

I could crack a whip at the lions
Although I'm afraid of the cat.
To the audience I'll wave
And pretend to be brave
And bow with a doff of my hat.

There's a circus coming to Brecon
And I'm packing my suitcase right now.
But my mother is mad,
And so is my dad,
And says that they will not allow.

54 Pride

Elspeth Smith was very poor,
a poor impoverished soul,
and she was quite ashamed of this,
and didn't want that role.

She lived with Mum in a faded house.
They struggled to survive,
Scrimping, saving every day
to try and keep alive.

But Elspeth Smith was oh so proud,
she didn't tell a soul
that when they had no food to eat
out came the begging bowl.

She bought her clothes from charity shops
and had done from the start.
She had the knack, and off the rack
she always looked so smart.

She was invited to a banquet.
Her Mother said, "Don't go,
Those people are too rich for us,
stick with what you know."

But Elspeth's eyes were gleaming,
an answer she did send.
She said, "I'd love to come my dears,
I certainly will attend."

She found the dress in London
in Portobello Road.
It needed alteration,
so Elspeth sat and sewed.

She added pearls and ribbons,
it was a lovely sight.
She got some pearly shoes as well
to dance away the night.

The banquet came and they all sat down,
it was a sumptuous fare
Elspeth's mouth was watering,
she could only stare.

Chicken, beef and poultry fine
on great big china plates.
Cakes and jellies, pastries,
apples pears and dates.

She ate her fill and drank the wine
and then thought of another,
feeling guilty sitting, eating
and not her starving Mother.

So when no one was looking
she filled her bag with stuff,
she rammed in beef and chicken.
She even filled her muff.

Then a man said, "Ladies
My friend has lost her ring,
a beautiful diamond cluster,
this is a dreadful thing."

"I'm afraid I must ask you ladies
to empty out your purse."
Elspeth paled and clutched her bag,
nothing could be worse.

The ladies emptied one by one

it came to Elspeth's turn.
She felt ashamed, how could she show,
her face began to burn.

Out came the beef and chicken too,
an apple and a pear.
Women gasped in horror,
and all the men did stare.

Then Elspeth ran right out the door
and fate did take its course.
A carriage crushed her pretty dress
she was trampled by the horse.

And if you've learned a thing or two
this one thing you must recal,
it does no good to be too proud
for it goes before a fall.

55   The Dying Woman

He gives me everything, except his time,
And everything's not worth a dime.
He cooks me scrambled egg on toast,
But takes away, what I want most.

With care he tends to all my needs,
He does not see how my heart bleeds.
He pats the quilt and offers tea,
It's nice, but he won't look at me.

My cheeks are pale, my hair like straw,
This creature now, he can't adore.
In sickness and in health they said,
On the day when we were wed.

But this long illness tests his mind,
He struggles 'gainst the ties that bind.
And when I die, he will be free,
Not bringing tea, reluctantly.

56 Father's Day

It's Father's Day and I have to say
I didn't send you a card.
To even think of Father's Day
I find extremely hard.
For you were never a father to me,
All my memories are bad.

Of awful sights and drunken fights,
A childhood, dark and sad.
You always smelled of drink you see,
I hated your rank breath.

And when you smashed the household up.
I longed just for your death.
I spent my nights in worry and stress
My daytime hours in shade.
Always nervous of your step
And very, very afraid.

I was small and young and vulnerable
You had me in your care
You treated me disgustingly
My life I could not bear.

I remember lying late at night
With my heart's irregular beats
When you came creeping in the room
Turning back the sheets.

I ran away but they fetched me back
And wouldn't believe my tales.
How you tore me from my grandmother's arms
Those years ago in Wales.

As my mother on her deathbed lay
She made you promise there,
That I would be looked after
With tender loving care.

And you lied and lied there on your knees
You didn't play your part,
But selfishly and brutally
You broke your daughter's heart.

So Father's Day is a joke to me,
A day I find quite hard.
So I'm sorry dear daddy
But you will not get a card.

57 The Belly Dance Lesson

"You can do it," I told her.
She was large and ungainly.
"It's hard to do," she said.
"I never realised it was so complicated."

"You just lift your hips up and down," I said.
"But to which wall?" she replied.
She continued,
"If there was a chalk mark on the floor,
What would it look like?"

I sighed and thought of brandy.
"You need a skirt," I said.
I looked at her jeans and clumpy shoes and sighed.
"You need sparkle and glamour, chiffon and silk,
Necklaces, earrings and bracelets,
Baubles and beads."

Her face looked blank,
"Can I bring the kids next week?" she said.

58   The Home

They put me in this place called home.
They wait for us to die.
Mothers, sisters, grandmothers, spinsters
All forgotten lie.

Those that feed us, do not love us,
Those that love us wait,
Visiting less often,
And this becomes our fate.

TV babbles rubbish
Endless cups of tea.
This person old, infirm and grey
What became of me?

59   Cat Lover

My cat is selfish, doesn't care,

Fixes me with evil stare.

Only follows me for food.

She's nasty, spoilt and very rude.

My cat is mean, too mean for words.

She chases mice, devours birds.

I've had this cat a long, long time,

Her friendship isn't worth a dime.

But I love her 'cos don't you see,

She condescends to live with me.

60 The Autumn Witch

The gusty wind blows
all the leaves in the wood.
The rain lashes down, wet and wild.

The autumn witch laughs
clinging onto her broom,
by this weather she is ever beguiled.

Her gown it is russet,
her hat green and brown,
with a cluster of fruit at its base.

Her hair is like fire
which sparkles and cracks,
whipping a storm round her face.

She flies through the trees,
she laughs and she sings.
She is the wild autumn witch.

She ripens the apples,
she browns all the nuts,
she brings you the colours so rich.

But as it gets colder
her gown it turns black,
and her hair seems the colour of earth.

The autumn witch fades
and dies like the leaves,
and awaits all the year for rebirth.

61   The Dancer

"I will dance for you," she said,
"At night, and the stars will shine anew.
With naked feet, I will twist and turn
Upon the evening dew.

And we will love under a waiting sky
On the grass beneath the trees.
I will give myself and let you do
Whatever you damn well please."

But I knew she lied and would never dance
For she loved another, true.
But she loved to tease and my heart to please
And there is nothing I can do.

This woman is my blood and bone,
Since we met, we have been one,
And I have stayed and hoped and prayed
When I really should have run.

And I want is to see her dance for me,
Spangles flashing on her skirts
And the thought that she may never dance
Saddens me and hurts.

One day my dancer will be gone
And I'll be left to cry.
My fleeting dancer of the woods,
Without her I will die.

62   Hannah Belle Crosses Over the Bwlch

Dear reader, have you ever wondered
While sitting in your abodes
Who it was who made them,
The Heads of the Valleys Roads?

Those narrow twisting little lanes
That wind in and out the mountains,
Passing sheep and forests,
Rivers, rocks, and fountains.

Well I'll take you back a long, long time,
Before the roads were there.
Walking was very difficult
And no one seemed to care.

It was hell to get to Cardiff
And I'll tell you something brother,
It could take months and sometimes years
To get from one valley to another.

Then a town all got together,
Each and every man,
Saying, "We must do something."
So they all devised a plan.

But as usual they did nothing,
And I'll show you all in verse,
How it took a gallant woman
To stop things getting worse.

One day into the valley
Rode a woman brave and strong.
She didn't intend to get involved
Or to stay for very long.

But she heard about the men
Who I've mentioned in these odes,
Who wanted nothing more in life
Than to have some decent roads.

This female's name was Hannah Belle
And she offered to do the job
For thirteen weeks free lodging
And an extra couple of bob.

So the town agreed to let her,
And the men they laughed real good,
And said, "Let her get on with it."
They didn't think she could.

Then Hannah went away for a while.
They didn't expect to see her again
Until one misty morning
She was stood there in the rain.

She had seventy-five pit ponies
And ten elephants behind them.
She asked for ropes and tackle
With which to tie and bind them,

Then she bought ten gallons of syrup of figs
To help her reach her goal.
Twenty-six tons of hazel nuts,
And tons of Welsh small coal.

Then she fed this to the ponies.
The men no longer smirked.
She slapped the rump of the nearest one,
And hoped the diet worked.

So the ponies trotted on at speed

Laying the road through the town,
And the elephants followed on behind
Tamping it all down.

She travelled many, many miles,
The road grew long and wide,
Pit ponies and the elephants,
With Hannah as their guide.

So Hannah took the credit
Which was so rightly hers.
The roads right over the mountains
Have been there for donkeys years.

So now you know how the roads were made,
Not by chauvinistic pigs,
But by Hannah and her elephants,
Small coal and syrup of figs.

63 That's Marriage

You'd kiss my hand
And touch my face.
Make me feel part
Of the human race.
Now of that look
There is no trace.
That's marriage.

You'd once walk for miles
Just to see me for an hour.
There'd be presents and dinner
And maybe a flower.
Now everything's awful
and boring and sour.
That's marriage.

I once was the woman
But now I'm the maid.
I'm scrimping and scraping
And so badly paid.
My first youthly bloom
Is beginning to fade.
That's marriage.

There was you, there was us,
It was fun, we were free.
You would give all the world
To just talk to me.
But now there you are
With the chair and TV.
That's marriage.

64   Albums

My Mother is the keeper of the archives.
She hoards old photos in albums
Hidden away in trunks.
Hoarded like treasures.

Baby photos and outings to the beach.
Our life down through the years.
Proud photos wearing cap and gown,
Brides and babies.

You should put them online I say
And back them up.
She smiles and nods and does nothing.

She secretly holds lonely vigils with these photos,
Remembering us, and how we were.

She worries we will throw them away when she dies.
We probably will.

65 Our Land

If there was a land
where every day was sunshine
I would take you there.

A far distant land
of palm trees swaying
and yellow golden beaches.

We could walk along the sands
holding hands
and I would kiss you eagerly
and we could beach comb for treasures.

If there was a land
where everything was white with snow
and every day was Christmas
I would take you there
and we could fall about laughing
with a silly brown dog.

And we could build a hut of logs
and you could love me gently
by the fire.

If there was a land
a Never-never land
where you and I could fly
holding hands
like children
I would take you there
and we could play the livelong day
amongst the stars
and rainbows made of fairy dust.
If there was a land.

66 Death

Death likes to make a stranger of your face.

It makes your features waxen.

It takes away your grace.

The undertaker pretties you up,

Stuffs your mouth with cotton wool.

Uses make up, prods and pokes

Till lips and cheeks are full.

Death likes to make a fool of you.

It takes away your light.

It makes you empty, vacant,

And not a pretty sight.

Once the spirit leaves its home,

For heaven or for hell,

Death has had the last laugh

as far as I can tell.

67   El Presidente

The hot sun struck
Swirls of dust
Disturbed by the horses' hooves,
Lifted from the desert floor.

Water splashed from the fountain
Making me thirsty.
I saw him come
His chest glittering with ribbons
And medals.

He strutted down the steps
Into my eyes.

Sweat trickled from my bandana
And I raised the gun
And shot him down
Releasing him from pretended honour,
From life itself.

I watched him die
And didn't know then he was my Father.
It would have made no difference.

68   A Hot Afternoon in Italy

The old lady knelt in front of the shrine
Hoping for tears of blood from the Madonna
Or at least a wink from the plaster eye.

She gazed at the holy relics.
St. Cyrus's toenail glinted
Benignly back at her.

She lit three candles for her dead sons.
She said three Hail Marys for her whoring daughters.
She straightened up,
Her back hurt.

She looked once again longingly at the plaster eye
Then limped from the church
Into the hot afternoon.

A stray cat, thin and emaciated crept near
She kicked it into the gutter.

69 Cat

I press my face against your black fur.
I breathe in earth and trees.
A tiny piece of bird down
Sticks in your claw
Giving you away.

A small cobweb covers your ear
and the dust of centuries
lies upon your paws.

I press your head to my face
Filling up my mouth with whiskers.

I place my head on your chest
And the steady rumbling purr
Like the thrumming of a great harp
Brings me peace.

I place my hand on your warm belly
And strong back legs
Pump it away.

You strain wildly and leap away
To sit licking unconcernedly
On the chair.

Your look of disdain withering.
Oh, I love you, CAT.

70 Confusion

I see the wrong that round me lies,
I feel the guilt within.
I struggle weakly 'gainst my ties,
I take no part in sin.

I wonder greatly at a God
Who turns his head away.
I spurn him ever in my head
Then clasp my hands to pray.

I tell myself, one life I've got
But really don't believe it.
I think of Hell and Heaven too
But really can't conceive it.

I ponder long upon a thought
That God's no longer there,
Until it rains amid the sun
And a rainbow curves the air.

71 Salute to Nature

Out of the door each morning,
To salute nature.
Watch each season,
The naked bough clothe itself
And the leaves each Autumn,
Russet tinted curl edged
Released from a season's burden.

And each Winter,
Feel the sting of white hoar frost
And the snow,
Muffling the world in its mantle.
See the trees,
Sentinels to the stars,
Reaching to sky's blue vault.

And in Summer,
See it all transpire.
I raise my arms
In silent Hallelujah.
The child facing confirmation
Can feel no more a sense of awe than I.

72   Fire Gazing

Imagine if you could go
Through the blazing portals of the fire.
Feeling no heat, no pain in your feet,
To dance amongst flames.

Imagine if you could go
Into the gold and orange depths,
With flames of blue and every hue,
And breathing hot breaths.

Imagine if you could go
Into the depths of a miniature Hell,
To walk upon coke, and mingle with smoke,
And live to tell!

73 Scared

It's hard to get back to the dating game
when you're fifty plus like me.
You see I've lost my confidence,
my lock has lost its key.

My skin no longer has its bloom
and all my bits are baggy.
I'm not into skirts that fit like gloves,
I go for loose and baggy.

I haven't kissed a man for years,
I'm sure I've forgotten how.
I used to be a sexy girl,
but where's that girl gone now?

I'd like a man who is good and kind,
one I'd like to know.
Who would take me out to dinner,
and just take things real slow.

It isn't that I'm scared of course,
but I've had my share of sorrow.
I'd like to start the dating game,
but not today - tomorrow.

74 A New Awareness

Birds have sung their hearts out this Springtime,
I never noticed much before.
The trees are thick with blossom this Springtime,
I never gathered it before.

The sun is stronger, the catkins longer.
Have other Spring times been so poor?
I seem to revel in the growing,
feeling lightness in my limbs.

Ever feeling, ever knowing,
seeing, hearing, nature's hymns.
This Springtime has been extra special,
taken to my heart to hold.

Something tells me it's my last one,
maybe I am getting old.

75 Men Don't Care

It's no good fussing with your hair,
'cos men don't care.
It's no good buying stylish clothes,
they want you bare.

You may wear shoes with style and flair
and you'll ask him straight
about your rear.

But I'm telling you
plain or fair,
Men don't care.

It's no good hoping he will stare
'cos men don't care.
It doesn't matter what you wear,
for him to notice would be rare.

He will not tell you,
he won't dare,
but he doesn't care.

You haven't got a hope or prayer,
do what you like,
but this I swear,
Men just do not care.

76 The Elfin Prince

Looking into the windows of your soul
I nearly drowned in there.
The deep blue grey flame that blazes there,
For freedom maybe?

Looking at your fine-drawn hands
I see they are strong
Yet gentle.

While making water lily flowers
Out of the table napkins
In the Indian restaurant.

I have been told that elves steal.
They take food and the cream off the milk.
I wonder what you will steal from me?

You show me your souvenirs
That you have collected on your travels.
You ask me to stay,
But I am afraid of elves
So I left,
Hurrying back to the Hotel.

77 One Book

To write great things is my desire.
Strong words to set the world on fire.
But everything, I feel I write
Seems to me, not worth a light.

Some of it, is weak and sad,
And some of it, seems not too bad.
But nothing sets the world alight,
And yet I still go on and write.

If only I could have one book
Published, lying in its nook,
In Smiths or Borders, any store
And people clamouring for more.

Just one, a small one on display,
For all to see, I might one day.
I swear I will, it will be read,
And I expect by then I shall be dead.

78   Who Can We Blame?

When things go wrong in your very young life
and you can think of no other person
you can blame for it all,
Blame your Mother.

When life turns out not the way you had hoped
and you want another,
here she stands to take the blame,
Blame Mother.

It's always Mother's fault you know,
she did neglect or smother.
She cannot win, she is full of sin,
Blame Mother.

Whenever you fail or end up in jail,
Don't blame your sister of brother,
here she stands to take the blame,
Blame Mother.

When you are off the rails and your marriage fails,
it's not your fault but others,
and there they stand the guilty ones,
the women who are Mothers.

And if you haven't got a Mum,
and was brought up by Gran or Nanny,
then it's OK, to turn round and say,
It's all the fault of Granny.

79 Take One of These Crowns

Take one of these crowns
I heard the Queen say,
And a necklace too, and a brooch,
And have some paintings and ornaments,
And sell my golden coach.

I've got all these castles I don't need.
I'm sure one will suffice.
So, sell the one that's in Scotland.
You're sure to get a good price.
Then give it all to the homeless,
The suffering, and the poor.

I'm old now, and I don't need it all.
I'm rich and that's for sure.
I want the people to love their Queen,
And let them know I care.
I don't need a royal yacht nor train.

I don't think that it's fair.
There are furs and dresses by the score,
I am more than ready to share.
I want my people to love a queen
That's true and just and fair.

I don't want to see people starving.
I can't bear to see them in need.
In fact, you can have the Crown Jewels.
Think of the people they'd feed.

80 Insomnia

I dread the thought of going to bed
To lay me down my tired head.
I need to rest and go to sleep
all night my lonely vigil keep.

My racing mind I cannot still,
cup of milk and take a pill.

The Sandman doesn't come my way
and jumping sheep refuse to stay.
It's time to rest my weary head
but I dread the thought of going to bed.

81 Men and Shopping

If one day you decide to go shopping
Thinking new clothes would be nice,
I have a little suggestion,
I have a little advice.

Don't take your husband out with you,
You will never get any of it done.
Shopping should be relaxing.
Shopping should also be fun.

Men just don't understand shopping
And will brag, "If I need a vest,
I buy in the first shop I come to,
No point in going to the rest."

You see them in Marks and Spencer
Looking lost with a glaze in the eye
While you look at twenty-five dresses
Deciding which one to buy.

Men just don't seem to get it.
Shopping gives you a high
Women go shopping for hours,
And men do not understand why.

So, save yourself grief and dejection,
For a man who likes shopping is rare.
He would rather have tea and the telly
And be sat in his favourite chair.

82 Reaping What You Sow

I went to my father's funeral today,
I can tell you I didn't want to go.
There was me and six other people,
Well, don't you just reap what you sow?

Only one of the six really knew him,
Through each decade, and all of the seasons,
They all were late comers in his long life,
There for a myriad of reasons.

If they had known him forever as I did,
Knew all the things I have known,
Saw the mistakes he had made in his life,
I would be at the graveside alone.

I still don't know why I went there,
I guess I needed to know he was dead,
Needed to close the book's chapter,
To forget the life he had led.

I cried though I didn't expect to,
But my tears were not for the dead,
But for the loss and the waste of my lifetime,
And all the things that were unsaid.

I'm at peace now he's gone, yes at peace,
Whether he is at peace we don't know,
He had never believed in a heaven,
Well don't you just reap what you sow?

83 The Devil's Silver Bell

Melinda awoke and discovered herself,
In a coach of blackest leather.
She couldn't make out how she came to be there,
In the foulest of all weather.

The lightning was flashing, thunder was rumbling,
The coachman stopped the coach.
Melinda stepped down, he threw down her bags,
And she saw a horseman approach.

He was an amazing sight to her
Upon his ebony steed.
His chest was bare, his black hair long,
And Melinda started to plead.

"Who are you?" In a trembling voice
"Tell me where is this place?"
"Why this is Hell," he roared at her,
Laughing down in her face.

"And I am the Devil, Melinda,
And you are one of my treasures,
And we shall spend eternal hours
Pursuing death's many pleasures."

He lifted her upon his horse.
The sky shone purple and green.
While flames danced crazily everywhere
Tinged with a golden sheen.

Then a palace appeared, a place so vast
It almost touched the sky,
And the devil threw Melinda down
And said, "I will say goodbye."

"I'll send for you when I'm ready
You will hear a silver bell.
For there's nothing to do but enjoy yourself

117

When you're here forever in hell."

So Melinda spent each passing week
At parties and at dances.
Gambling, cheating, lying,
Starting new romances.

She decided hell wasn't so bad
When you looked at it all together
Except you couldn't venture outside
Because of the terrible weather.

Then someone told her, didn't she know?
"When the lightning flashed above,
And the thunder roared in blue, black skies
'twas the devil making love."

"Then why hasn't he sent for me?" said Melinda.
"Why haven't I heard the bell?"
"Because there's a lot of women my dear
Waiting here in hell."

"But I'm so bored," said Melinda,
"I'm really bored to tears."
"But you've only been here for weeks my dear,
And you've got years and years and years."

"But when you're allowed to do all the things,
The things that shouldn't be done,
You find with repetition
They're no longer any fun."

"And the only thing to look forward to
In this awful place called Hell,
Is the thunder and the lightning
Of the Devil's silver bell."

"Have you heard it?" asked Melinda.
"Yes, I heard it sweet and low."
"When was that?" she asked her.
"Ten million years ago."

84 Juliette

She stood in her sparkling evening gown,
her wrinkled arms on show.
Her jewels sparkled in the light,
her age I did not know.

Once her dazzling beauty
had all men in her thrall.
She was feted everywhere she went
at all the grander balls.

The make-up, caked, was ghastly,
In the lines etched in her face.
Her shoes were worn, her gloves were torn
to a thread of tattered lace.

She stood upon the landing
looking old and frail,
then descended carefully,
her hand upon the rail.

She remembered her past glories
when she was wined and dined.
She was sick of being hidden away
out of sight and mind.

She didn't want to give it up
those days that were so heady.
They told her, "Grow old gracefully."
But Juliette wasn't ready.

She walked into the ballroom,
Her frail old head held high.
She waited for recognition,
her spirits lifted high.

But no one there acknowledged her,
standing full of pride.
For back in 1831,
Juliette had died.

85 Invisible

I feel invisible
Do you know that?
Like a wardrobe,
Or a chair, or a doormat.

When did you notice me last?
Can you remember?
Was it yesterday?
Last week, last December?

I feel insignificant,
Do you care at all?
You look right through me.
Come up against me, like a brick wall.

We were in love once,
And yes. You looked at me then.
Pity I can't have that time back
Once again.

I am invisible
I shall fade away
Like a vision, like a mist
Like an old day.

Will you even notice
That I'm no longer here.
Just some belongings
And some feelings, and a sad tear.

86 Lonely Christmas

I had a call from my son today,
And one from my daughter too.
They'll be very busy this Christmas,
There is nothing they can do.

They won't be coming for Christmas
And they apologised.
"Go to meet some friends instead"
Is what they both advised.

"That's fine," I said, "We do not mind,
Your dad will understand,
And yes, I'm sure we will miss you,
But on the other hand."

"Of course, it means less cooking,
And we can have a rest."
I smiled and joked and accepted it.
I think I passed the test.

But deep inside I felt so sad,
Wishing they were not grown,
And far too busy with their lives
And now we'd be alone.

Him and me at the table
With nothing much to say.
Watching rubbish on the telly
Just us on Christmas day.

What's the point of trimming a tree,
And making my mince pies.
If I said I didn't mind,
Well, I'd be telling lies.

87   Lost Property

In the land of lost umbrellas,
And the island of odd socks,
There are wonky legged tables,
And backward facing clocks.

The moon is out the livelong day,
The sun is out at night,
And single gloves and mislaid scarves
Are spoiling for a fight.

It's where they go when they are lost,
Where coats and keys abound.
All the things that are mislaid
And never will be found.

All the wallets and the purses
Hate it on their own,
And try to get into the box
That's for the mobile phones.

All the pens and pennies
Are in another box,
In the land of lost umbrellas,
And the island of odd socks.

88 Motor Racing

I hate motor racing,
The cars going around.
Trendy young men,
And the harsh revving sound.

And right at the end,
The men who are vain,
Stand on a podium,
Wasting Champagne.

The rich have the cars,
The ones with the cash.
And the ghouls they all gather,
And long for a crash.

They sit in the cars
While the engine just ticks,
In their helmets and shell suits,
What a load of Grand Prix!

89 Speak to Me

"Speak to me," says I.
"What about?" says you.
"Cabbages and kings,
All the things
You'd say when we were courting."

He gives a sigh, he cannot lie,
He'd rather be out with his mates.
"At least try," says I.

"I must go down to the potting shed,
There are things to do."
"Oh come to bed," says I.
"You used to try,
At least pretend to lie."

"What the hell's the matter with you?" says you.
"We used to make love such a lot," says I,
"But couldn't do it now."

"Not with the belly you've got."
"You're no film star yourself," says you.
"Oh be quiet," says I.

"But I thought you said speak to me?"
"God, I will never understand women."

90 The New Pen

Let us see how this new pen writes.
It is quite an elegant pen,
And writes quite well
Some leak you know.

But this elegant new pen
Writes better and better,
And will do to write
My suicide letter.

91   The Return of the Prince

As a child I was brought up on fiction,
Sleeping Beauty, Snow White and the rest.
In every tale was a dark, handsome prince.
He was always put to the test.

As a girl I watched lots of Hollywood films
Where the hero was dashing and gay,
Dark handsome men like Rock Hudson.
Well I said he was dashing and gay.

As a housewife I looked round for romance,
For heroes with muscles and looks,
And I found it, oh how I found it
In all of those Mills and Boon books.

But reality, God how it differed,
Modern man and romance do not mix.
I should have stayed with the stories
To get my emotional fix.

He will go out for his games and his beer,
Fall asleep in front of the box.
Snore every night like a farmyard,
While sleeping in bed in his socks.

But there is a new day a'dawning,
The Chippendales have arrived on the scene.
With music and sexy white uniforms.
With bodies all gleaming and lean.

It's true that this prince is more brazen,
Enough to make your heart leap.
Snow White would have choked on her apple.
Sleeping Beauty would not go to sleep.

Now it's our turn to slaver and ogle,
The prince has returned in a team,
And now at my age I can rant, I can rage,
And women can once again dream.

126

92 Nothing Ever Changes

How did we come to lose to the English?
How did we come to fall?
Because, instead of minding the battlements
You were designing an oblong ball.

How did they overtake us,
And make us less than slaves?
Because, when you should have been fighting,
You were drinking in the caves.

And when they were taking your women,
Giving us lots of hassle,
Where were you in thirteen twelve?
Playing darts in a draughty castle.

So I guess you've always been the same,
You lazy great Welsh sap.
For your never around when I need some coal,
Or to fix a leaking tap.

93 You

I want hot buttered toast
And a fire and a book.

I want daisies in grass
By a soft babbling brook.

I want wild stormy coves
With the sea, sand, and rocks.

I want silence and sunbeams
And the ticking of clocks.

I want rain on the glass
And the quick lightning flash.

I want custard and apples
And sausage and mash.

I want Fry's chocolate cream
And a room with a view.

But most of all darling
I simply want you.

94   Cat Hair

I am standing on the bus stop
Picking cat hairs off my coat.
I thought about my precious cat.
She is a cat of note.

But all my clothes are covered,
Chairs and carpets too.
But I just really love that cat.
Whatever can I do?

I can't buy black or navy blue.
Of dark clothes I am wary.
I did once have black trousers,
But now they're white and hairy.

I don't know what to do I'm sure
As on this cat I dote.
Standing on the bus stop,
Picking cat hairs off my coat.

95 Dai's Coming of Age.

With apologies to Longfellow's Hiawatha.

By the shores of Porthcawl Harbour,
By the shining big sea water,
Come the rugby boys a'tripping,
Looking out for someone's daughter.

Off the bus and into Chinese
Into pub and on the fairground
Little Dai and Big Wil Hopkin
Wearing bobble hat and scarf.

Wil Hopkin knows Dai's inexperience,
Introduces him to Brains SA,
By the shining big sea water,
On the shores of Butty Bay.

Drunken Dai hears sea gulls calling,
Wailing screaming on the seashore
"What is that?" he said, "Wil Hopkin,
What is that?" he cried in terror.

"That is but the English crying,
Talking in their native language.
Talking, scolding at each other.
They play the game and rarely win it."

Dai saw the sun go down that evening
Rippling round into the water,
On the shores of Porthcawl Harbour
By the shining big sea water.

Drunken Dai saw sun descending
Crying, "What is that Wil Hopkin?"

Good old Wil he answers saying,
"Once an English football player,

Chipped his nails and he got angry
Took the rugby ball and threw it
Up into the sky one morning
Down into the sea it tumbled

That's the ball that you can see there."
Dai saw the rainbow in the heavens
In the eastern sky the rainbow
Whispered, "What is that Wil Hopkin?"

 And the good Wil Hopkin answered,
"'tis the hearts of rugby players
Like the flowers of the forests
Like the daisies on the coal tips.

When on earth they fade and perish
They blossom in the heaven above us."
Dai saw the donkeys on the sea shore.
"What are those?" he begged Wil Hopkin.

"Braying creatures on the sea shore
By the shining big sea water."
Wil answered once again by saying,
"Those are referees of rugby,

Could be Irish, could be Scottish
Now you know, we call them donkeys."
In the pub that very evening
Little Dai once so angelic.

Sounds of music, words of wonder
"Oggy, oggy," said the barmaid

Learned some of the National Anthem.
Sospan Fach and old Cwm Rhondda.

Learned to argue when in beer
Learned to drink the Brains SA.
Of all these things Dai learned the language
Learned the names and all the secrets.

How the Chinese built their restaurants
How to run out without paying
How the players ran so swiftly
Like the comets in the heavens.

How was Megan in the chip shop?
How much was a bag of chips?
Learned of every bird its language
Where they hid themselves in winter.

Where they went for miners' fortnight
By the shores of Trecco Bay
Leaving all his childish pastimes
What a lovely marvellous day.

Grateful now to big Wil Hopkin
In his mac and in his Dai Cap
Arms round shoulders softly singing
Wil is homesick for his pigeons.

Dai knows it all by now by damn
Who's a lovely boy for him Mam?
Dai's no longer inexperienced
Now he is one of the boys.

96 Dai's Death

Dai Versity, a collier,
once toiled underground.
Ever keen and willing
to earn an honest pound.

Dai Versity had vision,
Dai Versity had flair.
He had a friend, Will Power.
They made an awesome pair.

Dai Versity was big and strong,
he always had a dream.
Whilst working in the coal dust,
whilst hewing at the seam.

Dai Versity was different,
he wasn't like the herd.
He loved to hear good music,
he loved the written word.

Dai Versity died coughing.
Dai Versity died young.
His last days spent in hospital,
coughing up his lung.

97 Funny Phone Calls

My sister's having funny phone calls,
What is wrong with me?
He asks about her underwear
In the middle of our tea.

She screams and cries and slams the phone,
Says he has got a nerve.
When I would like to speak to him,
This poor little perv.

He never asks about my sexy bras
Nor the colour of my pants.
It's only for my sister
That he grovels and he rants.

If I should answer by mistake
He asks for her by name,
And there I am all ready
To play his little game.

So any little pervert,
Who is out there, make my day.
I'd love your funny phone calls
And would know just what to say.

98 Twinkle

Blazing light struck my eyes,
A vision of white,
Tingled with gold.
Christmas Eve.

"I am Twinkle the Christmas Fairy,"
He said.
Tattooed fists clutched
The brandy glass.
He drunk it in one go.

"I grant you three wishes,"
He said,
Flicking cigarette ash on the floor.
Shafts of light spreading out
Wings beating the gasping air.

He left through the door,
I followed quickly.
Snow was falling, no footsteps,
Nothing moved in that still night,

Christmas Eve, fifteen years later.
A knock on my door.
Streams of bright light seeping.
I opened it.
A tramp tattered and dirty,
Old jeans, the same tattoos,
Blazing light strikes my eyes.
"I am Twinkle the Christmas Fairy,"
He said.

Joy floods my heart,
My mouth stretches in a smile.
A joyous smile of recognition,
A benediction.
And oh, the glory of the light.

99 Mrs Smith

By day she was plain Mrs Smith,
Was sister, mother, wife.
Caring for her family,
Struggling through her life.

Holding down a crappy job
Trying to make ends meet.
Chatting at the school gates
Looking smart and neat.

Cooking for her husband
Seeing to everyone.
Her days were pretty boring
When all is said and done.

But once a week her life took flight,
Nothing was the same.
She wore a sparkling costume,
She even changed her name.

She draped herself in chiffon veils
Displaying all her charms.
Wore pearls and rubies around her neck,
And bracelets on her arms.

She became another person,
A creature born of myth,
And no one would have recognised
Plain old Mrs Smith.

100   Youth Talks to Age

You're sitting there with your bitterness,
No music in your soul.
You've spent your whole life working,
Digging down a mine for coal.

Your life was one long hardship,
Spent coughing up your lung.
Tell me something Grandad
Were you ever young?

Did you laugh and go to parties?
Did you wear good clothes like me?
Did you holiday in summer?
Surfing in a foaming sea?

Did you spend your time in discos,
Taking girls home on your bike?
Did you waste your time and money,
On anything you like?

When you look at me as I am,
You see a song unsung.
So tell me something Grandad
Were you ever young?

When you see me spending money,
You think of all you missed.
You envy me my freedom,
All the girls you never kissed.

When death calls round to claim you,
On your gravestone will be hung,
A notice saying this man
Was never ever young.

101 Age Answers Youth

You're sitting there in your denim jeans.
Your music is too loud.
Your hair is long and shining,
You are young and strong and proud.

Your life is one big party,
For you to have and hold
But tell me something sonny,
Will you like it when you're old?

Will you still wear denim jackets?
Will you still ride motorbikes?
Will you still be quite so certain
Of what your body likes?

Will your hair be down your shoulders,
Not so shiny and quite grey?
Will you still be quite so sure
What to do and what to say?

And when your skin begins to wrinkle
And your back begins to fold,
Tell me something sonny.
Will you handle being old?

When you laugh at other people
And are impatient on the road.
When you take your youth for granted
Taking everything you owed.

When old age creeps upon you.
He will catch you off your guard,
And I'll tell you something sonny,
You will find it very hard.